The U.S. Constitution

Locating the Author's Main Idea

Curriculum Consultant: JoAnne Buggey, Ph.D.
College of Education, University of Minnesota

By William Dudley

Greenhaven Press, Inc.
Post Office Box 289009
San Diego, CA 92198–0009

Titles in the opposing viewpoints juniors series:

AIDS	The Palestinian Conflict
Alcohol	Patriotism
Animal Rights	Poverty
Death Penalty	Prisons
Drugs and Sports	Smoking
The Environment	Television
Gun Control	Toxic Wastes
The Homeless	The U.S. Constitution
Immigration	Working Mothers
Nuclear Power	Zoos

Cover photo: Helena Frost, Frost Publishing Group, Ltd.

Library of Congress Cataloging-in-Publication Data

Dudley, William, 1964–
    The U.S. Constitution: locating the author's main idea / by
William Dudley; curriculum consultant, JoAnne Buggey.
        p.   cm. — (Opposing viewpoints juniors)
    Summary: Demonstrates how critical thinking skills are used to
analyze differing views on questions of constitutional law.
    ISBN 0-89908-611-X
    1. United States—Constitutional law—Juvenile literature.
2. Critical thinking—Juvenile literature.   [1. United States—
Constitutional law.]   I. Title   II. Title: U.S. Constitution.
III. Title: Locating the author's main idea.   IV. Series.
KF4550.Z9D88 1990
342.73′02—dc20
[347.3022]   90-42328
                                                                            CIP
                                                                            AC

CONTENTS

THE PURPOSE OF
THIS BOOK

An Introduction to
Opposing Viewpoints

When people disagree, it is hard to figure out who is right. You may decide one person is right just because the person is your friend or relative. But this is not a very good reason to agree or disagree with someone. It is better if you try to understand why these people disagree. On what main points do they differ? Read or listen to each person's argument carefully. Separate the facts and opinions that each person presents. Finally, decide which argument best matches what you think. This process, examining an argument without emotion, is part of what critical thinking is all about.

This is not easy. Many things make it hard to understand and form opinions. People's values, ages, and experiences all influence the way they think. This is why learning to read and think critically is an invaluable skill. Opposing Viewpoints Juniors books will help

you learn and practice skills to improve your ability to read critically. By reading opposing views on an issue, you will become familiar with methods people use to attempt to convince you that their point of view is right. And you will learn to separate the authors' opinions from the facts they present.

Each Opposing Viewpoints Juniors book focuses on one critical thinking skill that will help you judge the views presented. Some of these skills are telling fact from opinion, recognizing propaganda techniques, and locating and analyzing the main idea. These skills will allow you to examine opposing viewpoints more easily.

Each viewpoint in this book is paraphrased from the original to make it easier to read. The viewpoints are placed in a running debate and are always placed with the pro view first.

Locating the Author's Main Idea

Authors include many ideas in their writing. But each sentence, each paragraph, and even each book they write should contain one main idea. For example, the main idea of this book is that the intent of the U.S. Constitution is a much-debated issue.

Locating the author's main idea, whether it is within the sentence, paragraph, or entire piece of writing, is a basic reading skill. It is important because it allows readers to identify the theme of an author's writing. It also allows readers to understand the main point an author is trying to make about the theme.

In this Opposing Viewpoints Juniors book, you will be asked to analyze specific paragraphs to locate the main idea. Sometimes the main idea is placed at the beginning of the paragraph. Sometimes it is placed somewhere within the paragraph, or even at the end. For example:

> People have destroyed the homes of many animals by cutting down trees in the rain forest to use for construction. They have also cut short the food supply of many grass-eating animals by using prairie land for building homes and businesses. People's use of the land is threatening the existence of many animals.

The main idea of this paragraph is placed at the end. It is that people's use of the land is threatening the existence of many animals.

When you begin reading the paragraph, you might think the first sentence is the main idea. If it is, then the other sentences in the paragraph will support it in some way. They might explain the idea more specifically or give examples or reasons.

Read sentence two. Does it do any of these things? No. In fact, sentence two is very much like sentence one. Sentence two even says *also*, which suggests that the two sentences are giving two ideas about the same topic.

Now read the last sentence. It is a general statement about the topic of destroying animals' habitats, while the first two are specific examples of this. The last sentence in this paragraph is the topic sentence. The other two sentences support this last sentence.

If you outlined this paragraph, it would look like this:

1. People's use of the land is threatening the existence of many animals.

   A. (Example 1) People have destroyed the homes of many animals by cutting down trees in the rain forest to use for construction.

   B. (Example 2) They have also cut short the food supply of many grass-eating animals by using prairie land for building homes and businesses.

Most paragraphs can be outlined in this way. By reading a paragraph carefully, you should be able to tell which sentence presents the main idea and which sentences explain or support it in some way. Outlining the paragraph may help you figure this out.

We asked two students to write one paragraph each in which they state their main ideas about the U.S. Constitution. Examine the following viewpoints to locate the main ideas.

I think the Constitution promotes equality.

The United States Constitution is one of the most important documents in the world. It established the first national government committed to freedom and equality for all of its citizens. Many things we take for granted, such as freedom of speech and the right to a fair trial, come from our Constitution. The people who wrote the Constitution were geniuses. Many other countries have copied parts of the U.S. Constitution in writing their own.

I think the Constitution hinders equality.

Does the Constitution really live up to the ideals of freedom and equality for all? The Constitution was written by wealthy white men. Many of them owned slaves, which the Constitution allowed. Women were not granted the right to vote until 1920. The Constitution does nothing to help poor people get jobs, homes or food. I think the Constitution does not protect many rights that should be guaranteed.

ANALYZING THE
SAMPLE VIEWPOINTS

Roy and Irene have very different opinions about the U.S. Constitution. Each presents one main idea in his or her viewpoint.

Roy:

MAIN IDEA

The Constitution is one of the most important documents in the world.

Irene:

MAIN IDEA

The Constitution is unfair to many people.

Roy's main idea comes at the beginning of his statement, while Irene's main idea comes at the end.

As you continue to read through the viewpoints in this book, remember to look for the main idea of the specified paragraphs.

1

PREFACE: Is the Constitution Elitist?

The United States Constitution was created in 1787 by a group of fifty-five delegates who assembled for four months in Philadelphia, Pennsylvania. They were facing a crisis. After winning independence from Great Britain in 1781, the thirteen former colonies were run like separate countries, not as part of a single nation. There was no national leader or system of courts. Trade between the states was difficult, and the economy suffered. In some states armed rebellion broke out against local governments. Revolutionary War leaders such as George Washington feared that the gains of the war for independence were being lost.

The delegates sought to establish a national government that would effectively govern the people. Yet the founders wanted to set limits upon the government's power. The result, after much debate, was the United States Constitution. Consisting of a preamble and seven articles, the document established the structure of the new national government and described the powers it possessed. After the states ratified the Constitution, it became the supreme law of the land and the foundation of a new national government.

The Constitution was at first very controversial. There were fierce debates in the states over whether it should be ratified. Following its adoption, however, it quickly became highly regarded as one of America's most important achievements. For some people the Constitution is the blueprint that enabled the U.S. government to live up to the ideals expressed in the Declaration of Independence.

Some critics, however, question whether the Constitution truly fulfills these ideals, especially whether it creates a government in which "all men are created equal." The Constitution, they argue, was written by an elite group of wealthy white men who considered others unfit to govern themselves. The result, critics say, was a Constitution designed to serve the founders' interests. Black slaves, American Indians, women, and people without property did not fare so well in the original Constitution. Some argue that women and minorities are still treated unfairly today under the Constitution.

The following viewpoints offer differing opinions on whether the U.S. Constitution protects all individuals. As you read these viewpoints, you will be asked to locate the authors' main ideas in specified paragraphs.

The Constitution is a magnificent achievement

Editor's Note: The following viewpoint argues that the United States Constitution successfully fulfills the ideals of freedom and equality described in the U.S. Declaration of Independence. It argues that the framers of the Constitution were dedicated to creating a government without tyranny and that the Constitution is an enduring work of genius.

The main idea of this paragraph comes at the beginning.

By most standards, the story of the United States has been one of success. Today the United States is one of the wealthiest and most powerful nations in the world. It is also one of the freest. People in America are free to elect and criticize their leaders. They have freedom of the press, speech, and religion. They are free from unjustified arrests and detentions by the police. Many peoples of the world, past and present, have not had and still do not have these freedoms.

What explains the success of the American experiment? One reason is our Constitution, which is a wondrous achievement. Phyllis Schlafly, a writer and political activist, argues that the U.S.

Constitution is "the fountainhead of the religious, political, and economic freedoms all of us enjoy in America." William Gladstone, a nineteenth-century prime minister of Great Britain, said "The American Constitution is the most wonderful work ever struck off at a given moment by the brain and purpose of man."

The Constitution was not without flaws. It was a product of its time. It did not eliminate slavery, and it did not grant women the right to vote until 1920. But by laying the foundations of democratic government and by giving the people the power of amendment, the Constitution has allowed for the correction of most of these flaws over the past two hundred years.

Which sentence best expresses the main idea of this paragraph?

Of course, the history of the United States has not always lived up to the ideals expressed in the U.S. Constitution. African-Americans, for instance, were deprived of fundamental rights until amendments were added after the Civil War. Even then, they were not treated as equals. But the Constitution played an important part in the Civil Rights movement. In 1954 the Supreme Court outlawed segregated schools as unconstitutional. With the Constitution and the Supreme Court behind them, civil rights leaders such as Martin Luther King Jr. led protests to ask for the end of segregation in schools, stores, and other places. King and others used their freedoms of speech and press to demand other fundamental rights already written in the Constitution. Civil rights leader Ralph D. Abernathy has argued that because of the Constitution, the fight for civil rights in the 1950s and 1960s might have been far more violent and less successful than it was.

Does the first or last sentence better express the main idea of this paragraph?

The greatness of the Constitution can also be seen in its international influence. Of the 170 countries existing today, 160 have written constitutions that were either influenced by or modeled after the U.S. Constitution. Oscar Schachter, professor of international law, argues that "the whole notion of human rights as a world-wide movement was grounded in part in the Constitution." For the past two centuries, people around the world have recognized that the U.S. Constitution is truly a remarkable achievement.

What is the author's main idea of this paragraph?

What makes the Constitution great?

How are the American people able to correct the flaws in the original Constitution according to the author? Does the viewpoint justify the Constitution's endorsement of slavery? How does it argue that the Constitution remains a great document even with that flaw?

Editor's Note: This viewpoint argues that the Constitution is elitist in several ways. First, it argues that the writers of the Constitution were rich men primarily concerned with protecting their own wealth. Second, it argues that the freedoms the Constitution supposedly protects are still not fully enjoyed by the poor and minorities. Finally, it argues that people should not depend on the Constitution to ensure their freedom and equality.

The main idea in this paragraph is stated in the first sentence.

The United States Constitution is not as great as many people think it is. Many people seem to think that the Constitution is some sort of sacred document. They believe it was written by immensely wise "founding fathers" that steadfastly protected the freedom of "we the people." These beliefs, if not wholly false, are not quite true either. If we look at the intentions of the framers of the Constitution and the effect of the Constitution on our lives today, we see that it did not create a truly democratic government.

First, let us take a closer look at the framers of the Constitution. They were all wealthy landowners, merchants, and lawyers who looked at the common farmers and townspeople (not

Of course we have a government of the RICH. You don't expect us to waste government on the poor, do you?

to mention the African slaves) with disdain and fear. The framers of the Constitution were primarily concerned with preserving their wealth from what they called the "mob" rather than extending democracy to all Americans. As one of the delegates, Roger Sherman of Connecticut, put it, "The people should have as little to do as may be about the government." In the words of current author and scholar Michael Parenti, "The intent of the framers of the Constitution was to *contain* democracy, rather than give it free reign." The people who wrote the Constitution were not interested in liberty or equality for the common people.

The Constitution's limitations concerning minority groups are especially easy to see. The Constitution did not grant any rights to black slaves. They were denied any vote or role in government. African-Americans were denied constitutional rights until the addition of the thirteenth, fourteenth, and fifteenth amendments after the Civil War. But even after these amendments were adopted, African-Americans would have to struggle and protest for another hundred years to fully secure their rights.

The struggle of African-Americans to find true equality in the U.S. Constitution shows that there is a difference between what the Constitution says and what it actually does. As historian Howard Zinn writes, "the Constitution is of minor importance compared to the actions citizens take." Whether we are talking about racial equality or freedom of speech, our actual liberties depend more on our actions than on the words of a document written two hundred years ago. Our liberties were not given to us by the Constitution but have been taken by the "mob" of common people the original framers feared.

This struggle continues today. As Zinn argues, "We risk the loss of our lives and liberties if we depend on a mere document to defend them." We should not celebrate the genius of the Constitution and its writers but rather continually work to make a truly democratic government that protects the freedom of *all* its people.

The main idea of this paragraph is stated at the end of the paragraph. It is that the writers of the Constitution were not interested in democracy for all.

Locate the author's main idea in this paragraph.

Library of Congress

Is the Constitution democratic?

What is the author's opinion of the framers of the Constitution? Do you think that the framers' wealth influenced the way they wrote the Constitution? Why or why not?

Why does the author think that the Constitution is limited? Do you agree or disagree?

Locating the Author's Main Idea

The following paragraphs each contain one main idea. Below each paragraph are three sentences, one of which best expresses the main idea of the paragraph. Circle the sentence that best expresses the main idea.

EXAMPLE: The Constitution has endured the test of time. It has lasted more than two hundred years. Over that time amendments have been added to it. But the main body of the Constitution remains basically unchanged.

    a. The Constitution is more than two hundred years old.
    b. The Constitution has endured.
    c. Amendments have been added to the Constitution.

The answer is b. The author's main idea is that the Constitution is enduring, or long-lasting. The other choices support or develop the main idea.

1. The Constitution was written by fifty-five white men. No women participated in the discussions. Women were not even guaranteed the right to vote until 1920. The United States has yet to elect a woman president. The Constitution does not represent women.

    a. The Constitution does not represent women.
    b. No woman has been elected president.
    c. Women got the right to vote in 1920.

2. After the United States Constitution was written, it had to be ratified by at least nine states. Getting the Constitution ratified was very difficult. Some heroes of American independence, such as Patrick Henry, spoke out against the Constitution. They argued that the Constitution made the national government too large and powerful. Supporters and opponents of the Constitution wrote opposing pamphlets and newspaper articles and debated with each other. Finally, on June 21, 1788, the Constitution was ratified.

    a. Some American heroes opposed the Constitution.
    b. The Constitution was ratified on June 21, 1788.
    c. Ratifying the Constitution was a difficult task.

CHAPTER 2

PREFACE: Should the Constitution Be Reformed?

The United States has the oldest written constitution still in effect. Other countries have had constitutions that have been suspended, dropped, or ignored. Many Americans have wondered whether parts of the Constitution have become outdated. The Constitution was written at a time when the United States was a small, isolated, agricultural nation. Today it is a large industrial superpower. Some people argue that because the United States has changed so much, its Constitution also needs changing.

One of the main features of the Constitution questioned by critics is the separation of powers. The people who wrote the Constitution were afraid of creating a tyrannical government. So they divided the government into three branches: the presidency, Congress, and the courts. The idea was to set up a system in which none of these three branches of government could become too powerful. But some modern political observers have argued that this system makes the U.S. government inefficient. They argue that the two elected branches of government—the president and the Congress—are often opposed to each other. The government is thus paralyzed until the president and the Congress can come to some kind of agreement. This is just one of the topics critics bring up concerning reform of the Constitution.

The following viewpoints offer differing opinions on whether the Constitution should be changed. As you read these viewpoints, try to find the main ideas in the specified paragraphs.

Editor's Note: This viewpoint presents a case for changing the Constitution. It argues that combining the legislative and executive branches would enable the U.S. to better govern itself and fulfill its role as a world leader.

The United States Constitution is a remarkable document, and the U.S. has prospered under it for over two hundred years. However, it is not without flaws. As the U.S. has changed from a small agricultural nation into a world leader and an industrial power, the Constitution's flaws have become more visible. Because the U.S. plays an important role in the world, the United States Constitution needs to be reformed to allow the government to work better.

One of the main features of our present Constitution is its separation of powers between the Congress and the president. The framers of the Constitution were extremely wary of giving too much power to one person or institution. So they made sure the Congress and the presidency shared the power for making and enforcing laws. Each branch was supposed to check the power of the other. For the first 150 years, this system worked fairly well. One reason was that the federal government's responsibilities were relatively small. Decisions made by the U.S. government had less effect on the world.

Since the 1950s, however, two developments have made the idea of the separation of powers, and thus the Constitution, obsolete. The United States has become a world superpower and, with its nuclear weapons, has the potential to destroy the planet. This means that actions taken by our government have become critically important to the whole world. The second development has been the rise of split-party government. In the past, the president and the majority of Congress were members of the same political party. But in most of the years since the 1950s, the president has been a member of one party, while the other party has controlled Congress. In five out of the last six presidential elections, a Republican has won the presidency, while Democrats have won majorities in Congress. This means that decision-making has become a battleground between Congress and the president.

Which sentence best expresses the main idea of this paragraph?

The main idea of this viewpoint is that the Constitution needs to be changed. Does this paragraph support this main idea? Why or why not?

For example, if the president wants to cut taxes and Congress does not, it is very difficult for a decision to be made. The Constitution is partly to blame for this problem.

Some people, such as novelist Gore Vidal, argue that the president has become too powerful. Vidal argues that the writers of the Constitution "would be horrified at our latter-day presidents, who have operated outside the law and beyond the reach of the people." But former president Richard Nixon, who resigned under charges that he was violating the Constitution, argues that the president has become too tied down by Congress. Nixon has written that the president should have full power as commander in chief to conduct foreign policy and not "wait on the 535 members of Congress to make the quick, tough decisions for him."

This conflict between the president and Congress could be solved by reworking some parts of the Constitution. Some people like Vidal argue that "we should get rid of the entire thing except for the Bill of Rights," and replace it with a parliamentary system in which the executive and legislative branches are combined. But others call for more modest changes. These changes could include allowing members of Congress to serve in the president's cabinet. Such an arrangement would force the Congress and the president to cooperate more than they do now.

Our Constitution is a great achievement, but that does not mean it should not be reformed. By blindly following our Constitution, we could be hurting America's future.

Is the main idea of this paragraph the idea that the president is too powerful? Why or why not?

Locate the author's main idea in this paragraph.

How have conditions changed?

This viewpoint argues that the United States and the world have changed since the Constitution was first written. What were some of these changes? Do you believe they outdate the Constitution? Why or why not?

The Constitution should not be reformed

Editor's Note: The following viewpoint argues that the U.S. Constitution is fine the way it is. It argues that good political leadership rather than tinkering with the Constitution is necessary for American government to function well.

This paragraph has several sentences that focus on changing the Constitution. Which sentence do you think expresses the main idea?

The people who wrote the Constitution made it difficult to change. An amendment to the Constitution needs to pass three-fourths of both the Congress and Senate; and then three-fourths of the states must approve it. They made it difficult for a reason: Changes in the Constitution should not be made without much discussion and debate.

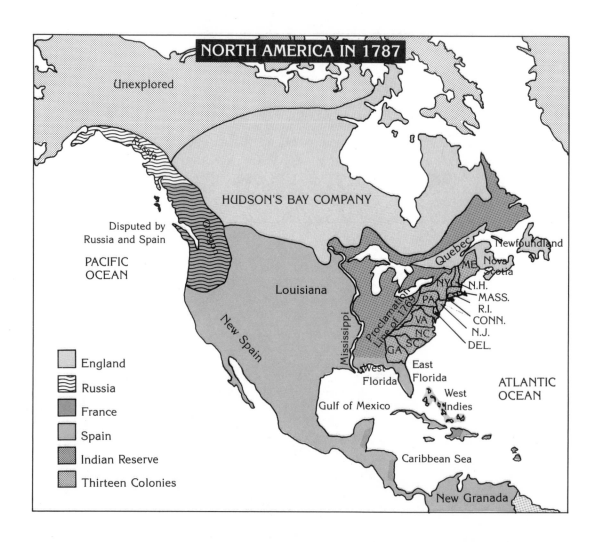

NORTH AMERICA IN 1787

Unexplored

HUDSON'S BAY COMPANY

Disputed by Russia and Spain

PACIFIC OCEAN

Louisiana

New Spain

Mississippi

Proclamation Line of 1763

Quebec

Newfoundland

ME

Nova Scotia

N.Y.

N.H.

MASS.

R.I.

PA

CONN.

VA

N.J.

NC

DEL.

GA SC

West Florida

East Florida

Gulf of Mexico

West Indies

ATLANTIC OCEAN

Caribbean Sea

New Granada

England
Russia
France
Spain
Indian Reserve
Thirteen Colonies

Some people have argued that the Constitution should be changed. They have claimed that the original framers were so afraid of tyranny that they put too many "checks and balances" in our government for it to function properly. But I think the framers' concerns about concentrating too much power in one place are just as valid today as they were then. We should not allow the president—or anyone else—to have too much power.

Some people believe we should have a parliamentary system like the one in Great Britain. In Great Britain the prime minister has control over both the executive and legislative branches, and can push through his or her ideas into law. But some government officials in England worry that the Parliament has too little control over the prime minister. They argue that the prime minister ends up acting like an absolute monarch. The historian Arthur Schlesinger Jr. has written that these reformers "yearn for a separation of powers" such as those written in the U.S. Constitution.

Instead of blaming our government for inefficiency, we should blame our political leaders. As Warren Manshel, former U.S. ambassador to Denmark, put it, "The Constitution treats us like adults. It asks that we be capable of working out our differences." Tinkering with the Constitution distracts us from what we truly need—effective political leadership. Our government officials should be wise enough to create and promote solutions within the constitutional system.

Changing the Constitution, according to former congressman John B. Anderson, could raise false expectations. If the perceived problems of government did not improve, the American people might be tempted to change the Constitution again . . . and again. The Constitution would lose the special place it holds in American hearts if it is changed too much or too often. We should try to work within the Constitution rather than try to destroy it.

The Constitution has served us well for the past two hundred years. I think it will be just fine for two hundred more. I agree with Schlesinger when he says, "I like the Constitution basically the way that it is." The Constitution does not need changing.

Locate the main idea of this paragraph.

Which sentence in this paragraph about the British Parliament expresses the main idea?

What is the main idea in this paragraph?

Locate the main idea in this paragraph. Do the remaining sentences support the main idea? Why or why not?

Does the Constitution need changing?

This viewpoint argues that the Constitution should not be changed. What reasons are given in support of this opinion?
    What does the viewpoint say about the British system of government?

Selecting the Main Idea

All paragraphs have a main idea and sentences that support that idea. Sentences that express the main idea are usually, but not always, found in the first sentence of the paragraph. Sentences that support the main idea give examples, statistics, and other evidence.

Below are several lists of sentences. Each list contains sentences about the same general topic. One sentence would make a good main idea, while the others could be used to support it. Circle the sentence you think best expresses the main idea.

EXAMPLE:
  a. Many leaders from other countries have admired the Constitution.
  b. For over two hundred years the Constitution has provided the basis for the U.S. government.
  c. The Constitution is a magnificent achievement.
  d. The Constitution has helped unite the diverse people who have settled in America.

The correct answer is c. The other sentences give supporting evidence or further expand on the statement that the Constitution is a great achievement.

1. a. The U.S. has grown much since the Constitution was written.
  b. The U.S. population was only four million in 1787.
  c. The number of states has grown from thirteen to fifty.
  d. Unlike it was in 1787, the U.S. today is a world superpower with great international influence.
  e. Today the U.S. population is over 240 million.

2. a. Over ten thousand amendments to the Constitution have been proposed since 1787, but only twenty-six have been adopted.
  b. Amending the Constitution requires two-thirds of both houses of Congress.
  c. Amending the Constitution is a long and difficult process.
  d. Three-fourths of the states must approve amendments passed by Congress.
  e. Some scholars believe the framers of the Constitution wanted changes to be difficult in order to ensure that only necessary ones were made.

3. a. The Constitution originally endorsed slavery.
  b. The Constitution said each slave was to be counted as three-fifths of a person in the national census.
  c. Prior to 1808, the Constitution forbade the making of any laws forbidding slavery.
  d. Delegates from the southern states fought hard to protect slavery.
  e. The Supreme Court ruled in 1857 that under the Constitution, black slaves were not to be considered as citizens with constitutional rights.

3

PREFACE: Should the U.S. Hold Another Constitutional Convention?

The United States Constitution can be changed in two ways. One is to have an amendment passed by two-thirds of both houses of Congress and three-fourths of the state legislatures. The first ten amendments, also known as the Bill of Rights, were added to the Constitution in 1791. Since then sixteen more amendments have been added. The most recent amendment was enacted in 1971 to give eighteen-year-olds the right to vote.

The only other way to change the Constitution is to hold a constitutional convention. If held, each state would select delegates who would then meet for the sole purpose of revising the Constitution or even creating a new one. According to Article V of the United States Constitution, a new convention could take place if two-thirds of the states request one. There has been no constitutional convention since the original one in 1787. However, thirty-two states, two short of the number needed, have requested a constitutional convention in order to add a balanced budget amendment.

The present Constitution is vague on whether a new convention can be limited to adding just one amendment or whether it can completely rewrite the Constitution. Many people worry that some states might use a new convention as an excuse to rewrite the Constitution. They argue that the U.S. should stay with the amendment process rather than risking the Constitution with a convention.

The following two viewpoints argue whether or not the U.S. needs a new constitutional convention.

The U.S. should hold a new constitutional convention

Editor's Note: This viewpoint argues that a new constitutional convention would be good for the U.S. It argues that changes in the Constitution are necessary and that the American people have the wisdom to change the Constitution for the better.

The United States Constitution states that a second convention can take place if two-thirds of the states request it. Currently, thirty-two states have called for a new convention in order to pass a balanced budget amendment. Only two more states are needed for a second convention to occur. Some people are alarmed by this situation. But there are several reasons why a second constitutional convention would be good for the U.S.

One good reason for a convention is the need for a balanced budget amendment. Our government's inability to stick to a national budget has reached a crisis stage. Our national debt has reached almost three *trillion* dollars. This is a figure that I am sure would have boggled the minds of the writers of the Constitution.

Congress has been unable to solve this problem. For the past ten years Presidents Ronald Reagan and George Bush have been calling on Congress to pass a balanced budget amendment that could then be submitted to the states for approval. But Congress, the source of the problem, has refused to consider one. We need to bypass Congress and change the Constitution with a new convention.

What is the main idea of this paragraph? Do all the other sentences support the main idea? Why or why not?

Which sentence best expresses the main idea?

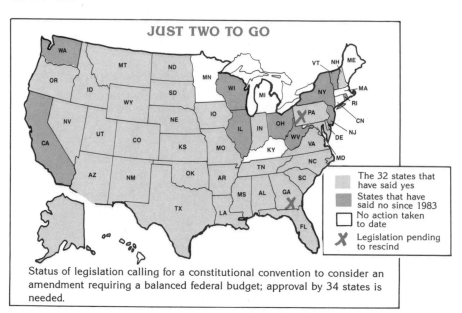

JUST TWO TO GO

The 32 states that have said yes

States that have said no since 1983

No action taken to date

X Legislation pending to rescind

Status of legislation calling for a constitutional convention to consider an amendment requiring a balanced federal budget; approval by 34 states is needed.

John T. Noonan, a professor of law and a constitutional scholar, offers another good reason for a new convention. He argues that the Supreme Court, which is supposed to interpret the Constitution, has become too powerful. He writes that the Court is making "new policy, new constitutional provisions," something it is not supposed to do. Good examples include the Court's 1962 decision outlawing prayer in public schools and its 1973 decision removing federal abortion laws. Should nine unelected judges have unrestricted power to change the Constitution? Or should these decisions concerning the budget, abortion, and other issues be in the hands of the people? Noonan argues that such important issues should be left to the people, and I agree. That is why we need a new convention—so the people, not the Supreme Court, can discuss and decide these issues.

What is the main idea of this paragraph? Is there one sentence that best expresses it?

Some of those who oppose a new Constitution believe the American people are stupid and that they may decide to get rid of freedom of the press, the right to a fair trial, and other constitutional freedoms. But I have more faith in the American people than they. Americans value their freedoms as much now as before and would not decide to drop them. Besides, decisions by the convention would have to be passed by three-fourths of the states, so any radical changes would be hard to push through.

No one sentence seems to state the main idea. What point is the author trying to make in this paragraph?

A new constitutional convention would get people more involved in their nation's welfare than ever before. Today only a few people know exactly what is in the Constitution. Less than half of our citizens vote in national elections. But a new convention would spark interest in our country and its government. Delegates undoubtedly would include people of every race, creed, and color, unlike those at the original convention, and ensure a fairer Constitution. Reexamining our fundamental values and freedoms would be good for America.

Does the author's main idea in this paragraph support the main idea of the viewpoint? Why or why not?

Is a constitutional convention necessary?

What main reasons does the author give in favor of holding a new constitutional convention?

According to the viewpoint, why is there little danger that a convention would drastically alter or limit the Constitution? Do you agree?

Editor's Note: The following viewpoint argues that a new convention would jeopardize the U.S. Constitution. The viewpoint states that a new constitutional convention should be held only in a time of crisis and that such a situation does not exist now.

The United States Constitution is under a threat that few people know about. The threat is the possibility of a second constitutional convention. If two more states join the thirty-two that have already called for one, then a new convention will have to be held. A new constitutional convention would be a bad idea for several reasons.

Locate the author's main idea in this paragraph.

One is the danger of a "runaway" convention. A convention might be called for in order to, say, pass a balanced budget amendment. But there would be nothing to legally stop delegates from making any other changes to the Constitution. They might choose to limit freedom of the press or the rights of suspected criminals. Walter Dellinger, a law professor, writes that "It would be impractical or impossible to limit the convention to one proposal." A convention would leave our Constitution vulnerable to drastic change.

© Graham/Rothco. Reprinted with permission.

Another reason a new convention would be dangerous is the presence of television and other media. The 1787 convention was held behind closed doors. This enabled delegates to speak honestly and frankly and to work out their disagreements in private. But such a situation would not exist now. Delegates would have to work under the full glare of television and newspaper coverage; even hearings would perhaps be televised. Delegates would find it difficult to make wise and careful decisions under such conditions.

Scholar and professor Mortimer J. Adler opposes a new constitutional convention for two more reasons. One is the difficulty of assembling a group of delegates that could compare to such original delegates as James Madison, Alexander Hamilton, and George Washington. In addition, Adler believes that the American public might not be educated enough to appreciate or vote wisely on a new Constitution. "A radical reform of basic schooling in the United States would have to precede any attempt by any means to improve our . . . Constitution," he writes.

Changes to the Constitution are much better made through the amendment process. Amendments are limited to one change at a time. This ensures that the rest of the Constitution will not be placed in jeopardy.

Why did the framers create the possibility of a convention in the first place? They did so in case the original Constitution was a total failure and the nation was in crisis. But the Constitution was not a failure. It has served us well for more than two hundred years. There is no crisis that justifies a new convention.

In conclusion, I agree with Harvard law professor Lawrence H. Tribe when he says that attempts to convene a constitutional convention are "irresponsible, profoundly misguided, and likely to precipitate a constitutional crisis." We should not play dice with our Constitution by calling a new convention.

Which sentences in this paragraph give additional information about the main idea?

What is the main idea of this paragraph?

Does the main idea of this paragraph support the main idea of the viewpoint? Why or why not?

What are the risks of a new convention?

Why does the viewpoint argue that a new constitutional convention will be risky? What is at stake?

The viewpoint argues that the American people and their leaders might not be educated enough to improve the Constitution. Do you agree or disagree?

3

Identifying the Main Idea in Editorial Cartoons

Throughout this book, you have seen cartoons that illustrate the ideas in the viewpoints. Editorial cartoons are an effective and usually humorous way of presenting an opinion on an issue. Cartoonists sometimes express their main ideas directly. Sometimes they let the readers determine the main idea of the cartoon by observing clues given in the words and illustrations.

Look at the cartoon below. From the cartoon's caption, what do you think the cartoonist thinks of a new constitutional convention? How can you tell? What other clues are in the cartoon that support your answer?

For further practice, look at the editorial cartoons in your daily newspaper. Try to decide what main idea the author is expressing in each cartoon.

"First thing to do is toss out a lot of this stuff adopted by the previous Convention."

Copyright 1979 by Herblock in *The Washington Post*

CHAPTER

PREFACE: Is Burning the Flag a Constitutional Right?

In 1989 the Supreme Court, in a five-to-four ruling, overturned the conviction of a political protester brought to trial because he had burned the American flag. The Court's majority ruled that burning the flag in protest was a first amendment right guaranteed by the Constitution. In June 1990, the Supreme Court reaffirmed its decision, again by a five-to-four vote, by striking down a law passed in Congress that made burning the flag illegal. The controversy continues as President George Bush and others now propose amending the Constitution to contain an article making flag-burning illegal. If the amendment were to pass, the Supreme Court would not be able to rescind it.

This controversy calls into question highly charged arguments about patriotic feelings vs. freedom of expression and what, if any, limits our original founders would have placed on freedom of speech. William Brennan, in the 1990 majority opinion, made a stirring argument in favor of protecting the right to burn the flag: "The bedrock principle underlying the First Amendment . . . is that the government may not prohibit the expression of an idea simply because society finds the idea itself offensive or disagreeable." Justice Anthony Kennedy added that recent revolutions in Eastern Europe in which flags were burned prove that this is an "internationally recognized form of protest."

People who support making it illegal to burn the flag believe it is the epitome of disloyalty and find the act despicable. They believe that making flag-burning illegal would protect not only the flag but all of the things it stands for. In the dissenting opinion, Justice John Paul Stevens spoke for many who take this position: "The flag uniquely symbolizes the ideas of liberty, equality, and tolerance . . . ideas that Americans have passionately defended and debated throughout our country." To Justice Stevens and others, the flag is a symbol that must be revered. Tolerating its destruction is tantamount to allowing citizens to openly attempt destruction of the United States.

Whatever the outcome of a flag-burning amendment, this debate has sparked many of the most fundamental emotions people hold about their country and their freedoms. The following viewpoints discuss this issue.

Editor's Note: This viewpoint argues that while burning the American flag may be a despicable act, the Constitution gives people the right to do it. It argues that making flag-burning an exception to free speech protections would weaken the Constitution and reduce the freedoms of American citizens.

The main idea of this paragraph is in the form of a question. How does this affect the point of the paragraph?

Which sentence best expresses the main idea of this paragraph?

This is a tricky argument to make. How can one be a patriotic American who loves the flag, yet still agree with the Supreme Court's ruling that burning the flag is protected under the First Amendment? It may be tricky, but I will try because this is exactly what I believe.

The key to understanding the position is to know the difference between *symbol* and *substance*. The flag is a *symbol* of the United States and the freedom it stands for. Other than that it is just a piece of colored cloth. But our Constitution is the *substance* of our freedom. It is the written law that limits our government and protects our freedoms. The Supreme Court in their flag-burning decision had to choose between protecting the symbol of our freedom and its substance. They chose, wisely I believe, substance.

© Swann/Rothco. Reprinted with permission.

Journalist Hendrik Hertzberg makes the same point in a slightly different way. Suppose someone who dislikes something in the U.S. Constitution decides to protest by burning a copy of it. Is the Constitution thus destroyed? No, because only a copy has been burned. Hertzberg says the same situation applies to the American flag. Someone who burns a flag does not destroy it, but only a copy. The true flag exists in the hearts and minds of the American people.

However, the Constitution can be damaged, according to Hertzberg, "by amending it in ways foreign to its spirit and hostile to its purposes." And this is what the flag-burning amendments that some people want all do. A flag-burning amendment would be the first amendment that would *limit* the freedom of speech guaranteed in the Bill of Rights of the Constitution.

Is flag-burning a form of speech? It is in a broad sense. It expresses certain feelings and opinions about America. If flag-burning was not speech, then people would not find it so offensive. The Constitution should protect all forms of speech, not just newspaper editorials or political debates.

I disagree with people who say the Constitution should protect all speech *except* for burning the American flag. My question is: If we make an exception now, where would it lead? Freedom of speech, *except* for people who insult our country? Who offend women and minorities? Who are different?

Oliver Wendell Holmes Jr., who was chief justice of the Supreme Court, said that true freedom includes freedom "for the thought we hate." This should include, if necessary, flag-burning. Our flag deserves protection, but our Constitution deserves even more.

Locate the author's main idea. Can it be written as a single sentence?

What is the main idea? Do the remaining sentences support it? Why or why not?

Which sentence best expresses the main idea of the paragraph?

The flag and the Constitution

What distinctions does the author make between the U.S. flag and the U.S. Constitution?

The viewpoint argues that the Constitution deserves more protection than the flag. Do you agree? Do you believe both should be protected equally? Why or why not?

Editor's Note: This viewpoint argues that burning the flag is not a form of speech that should be protected by the Constitution. It argues that the Constitution should be amended, if necessary, to protect the American flag.

What is the main idea of this paragraph?

The American flag is an important symbol of our nation. People have died for the flag. Millions of Americans are moved by the sight of it. As Chief Justice William Rehnquist put it, the flag "has occupied a unique position as the symbol of our Nation, a uniqueness that justifies a governmental prohibition against flag-burning."

Unfortunately, Rehnquist was in the minority as the Supreme Court ruled that flag-burning should be protected by the Constitution. By doing so, the Court did away with the laws in forty-eight states that made flag-burning a crime. This unfortunate ruling mocks both our flag and our Constitution.

The Supreme Court majority argued that burning the flag should be considered speech, and that freedom of speech is

"DESECRATION OF THE FLAG, A HANGING OFFENSE? REALLY, BEN...WE'RE RUNNING OUT OF SPACE! BESIDES...EVERY AMERICAN HOLDS THE FLAG TO BE AS SACRED AS THEIR MOTHER!"

Ed Gamble. Reprinted with permission.

protected by the Constitution. But what did the writers of the Constitution mean by freedom of speech? Did Benjamin Franklin and James Madison think they were endangering the American flag? Madison spoke of "the people's right to speak, to write, or to publish their sentiments." If these sentiments include a hatred of America, then people should be free to shout "I hate America." But they should not be free to go beyond words and actually burn the American flag.

Is there one sentence that best expresses the main idea of this paragraph? Why or why not?

Even if burning the flag can be considered speech, the right to freedom of speech is not unlimited. We do not allow people to yell "Fire!" in a crowded theater. We do not allow people to spraypaint slogans on the Washington Monument or on public buildings. Burning the flag is a sick, violent act. It deeply hurts the many Americans who love this country and its flag. They should have the right to outlaw flag-burning if they choose.

Locate the main idea of this paragraph. Do the rest of the sentences support this idea?

Some people have suggested amending the Constitution. One proposed amendment simply states: "The Congress and the States shall have power to prohibit the physical desecration of the Flag of the United States." A flag amendment like this will not affect free speech rights in any fashion. It does not weaken the rest of the Constitution. It simply protects the flag that is dear to so many patriotic Americans.

Does the paragraph's main idea support the main idea of the viewpoint?

Every country has the right to protect its flag, whether from foreign enemies or from sorry protesters. This principle should be as obvious as the rights of life, liberty, and the pursuit of happiness. Those who would set the Constitution against the flag do them both injustice. The freedoms of speech the Constitution protects should not be twisted to justify the trashing of our flag.

What is the main idea of this paragraph? Is there one sentence that best expresses it?

The flag and freedom of speech

The viewpoint argues that burning the flag should not be protected by the Constitution's guarantee of freedom of speech. What arguments does the viewpoint provide to support this position?

What are your feelings about the American flag? Do you agree with the statements in this viewpoint?

Developing the Main Idea

Below are seven topic statements. Each is related to the information you have read in the preceding viewpoints. Choose one and make it the main idea of a paragraph you write.

EXAMPLE: Topic: A flag-burning amendment is a bad idea.

A flag-burning amendment is a bad idea. The Constitution should be changed only if the nation is in crisis. But we have no epidemic of people burning the flag. Even if we did, does that create a real crisis for this country? A new amendment is unnecessary. It would also be harmful because it would set limits on what some people think is the most important part of the Constitution—the Bill of Rights. These original amendments to the Constitution spell out our freedoms, including the freedom of speech. A flag-burning amendment would set a precedent by limiting our freedoms.

1. Every U.S. student should learn about the Constitution.

2. The Supreme Court was wrong in allowing flag-burning.

3. The Constitution is outdated.

4. A second Constitutional convention should not be held.

5. Many countries admire America's Constitution.

6. The Constitution is unfair to women and minorities.

7. The Constitution is fair to women and minorities.